Self-Esteem

How To Rewire Your Brain To Replace Negative
Thoughts With Positive Thoughts And Improve Your
Ability To Love Yourself

*(Take Control Of Your Life Is A Course That Will Teach You
How To Do All Of Those Things)*

Coleman Evans

TABLE OF CONTENT

Introduction 1

When Should You Play The Part Of An Extrovert? 6

The Numerous Advantages Of Increasing One's Self-Confidence 12

How To Keep Yourself Motivated In Smart Ways 19

Is Having A Low Self-Esteem A Problem For Your Mental Health? 31

What Compels Me To Write This Book? 40

Let Go Of The Need To Be Perfect 49

Altering Feelings Via Behavioral Modification 65

Acquire A Sense Of Your Own Value. 85

Changes In Lifestyle To Foster Empathy 90

Developing An Optimistic And Upbeat Attitude 101

Having A Healthy Sense Of Self-Worth Makes One More Resilient In The Face Of Adversity And Pressure. 110

Move In The Direction Of Motivation 114

You Will Experience More Joy And Contentment In Your Life. 125

What Separates Self-Esteem And Confidence From One Another 134

The Importance Of Developing Good Habits For Keeping Your Emotions In Check 144

Introduction

The unexpected may and will happen in life. When children are growing up, their parents have the goal of helping them become independent and self-assured people. However, this goal may often result in the child's perception that they fall short of meeting their parents' expectations. However, this is not the end of the story. When navigating the labyrinth of relationships, you may emerge on the other side with emotional scars and very little confidence as a result of experiences such as betrayal or a shattered heart. You put your faith in life, and it humiliated you by betraying it. On the other hand, you are not the only one. Millions of individuals all around the globe are affected by the same kinds of difficulties, yet it manifests itself in a variety of unique ways for each individual. Some would shrink back, while others might spring forward. The fact that you are inspecting the pages under the cover of this book gives me the impression that you are making an effort to break out from the rut of being unhappy with who you are. No matter what may have occurred in the past, there is no need for you to feel awful about yourself at all. The reason you feel this way is because you made the decision to bring the baggage from your previous life into the one you are living now, and regrettably, you have acquired the habit of looking back on your life with emotions of regret. This is the reason why you feel this way.

Your sense of self-worth might suffer serious setbacks during your lifetime. Someone rips the rug out from under your feet just as you think you have everything under control, and all of a sudden, your world is flipped completely upside down. There are a lot of individuals out there who don't like themselves, and all of this is a reflection of how other people have treated them and how they have themselves interpreted this behaviour. You may be shocked at just how many people feel this way. It is not a simple chore to leave all of that behind you if you want to improve your self-confidence, but you have to do it. On the other hand, there are things that you can do to make you feel better about who you are, to accept yourself — flaws and all — and to continue to achieve in your life, just as every other person in the world is allowed to do.

This book was developed as a consequence of the author's experience helping individuals who lacked self-confidence and seeing their subsequent growth. I reasoned that if I were to disseminate information about these successful situations and demonstrate to readers how to boost their self-assurance, there could be some satisfied readers in the world who would benefit from the book. This book is for anybody who struggles with self-consciousness or lacks confidence and attempts to guide you through the process of developing that confidence. It is something that can be applied to everyone who struggles with these issues. You will be given certain assignments to do, all of which have been shown to boost levels of self-confidence. By the time you reach the conclusion of the book, you should have a more positive outlook on who you are and how you portray yourself to the outside world.

You will also get an understanding of how the level of your self-esteem impacts each and every connection you have, as well as the reasons why it might occasionally reduce the quality of your life. If your expectations are lower than what is reasonable for a human person, you should not be surprised if you get less than that. If, on the other hand, you modify your ideas and begin to accept yourself as you are, you have the same potential as anybody else to acquire the self-assurance you need to go through life in a manner that is more conducive to happiness.

When Should You Play The Part Of An Extrovert?

There may be moments when you have to put on an extraverted persona in order to accomplish particular tasks. When working on initiatives that are meaningful to you or to the people you care about, you should follow this practise. However, there are a few pointers that you need to keep in mind if you want to avoid feeling stressed out when you behave like an extravert.

Locate the undertaking that requires your attention the most.

To begin, you need to give some thought to the project that you will be working on later. You must choose where the project will begin and where it will come to a close. You should also determine the required measures that you need to do in order to bring the project to a successful conclusion.

Acquire the necessary proficiencies.

The next step that you have to do is to determine the extravert abilities that you will need to make use of. It is possible that you may be asked to network with new people or sell something to individuals. If your job include managing other people, you will likely be responsible for guiding them through the whole of the project.

You could, at times, be expected to exhibit a more outspoken personality. You will be required to speak with more individuals. There may be instances when you have to entertain folks that you have a cursory familiarity with. Even though these are not activities that introverts often engage in, you will need to engage in them in order to complete critical tasks.

Delegate responsibilities that you are capable of delegating.

If you are in a position of authority, you may want to consider delegating extraverted responsibilities to genuine extraverts, who, due to the nature of their personality, are more prepared to do the work. You need to recognise the fact that there are certain responsibilities that do not require your personal participation.

If the circumstances need it, you should do the extravert-type chores yourself. There will be instances when you do not have any extraverts who are qualified to do the assignment for you. There are other situations in which the responsibilities are not suitable to be assigned due to their level of significance.

Make the most out of a limited time.

When working on assignments that need you to have the outgoing demeanour of an extrovert, you need to get a head start so that you may wrap things up as fast as possible. When others want us to be someone other than who we are, we find it much easier to get exhausted. We start to be aware of all that we are doing. There are instances when we could experience awkwardness. The mind might get fatigued from having to constantly reflect on the behaviours that we carry out. If you are just starting out with a job that requires extravert skills, you may find that you need to complete it as quickly as possible to avoid mental exhaustion.

You should become better at the extraverted talent that you will be using regularly.

Our occupations need us to make frequent use of some extroverted talents, such as public speaking and networking. For instance, if you are in the sales industry, you must consistently interact with new individuals in order to generate sales leads. As a lawyer, you are required to make regular trips out into the community to meet with clients.

Determine the extraverted skills that are necessary for the success of your job and work towards developing such skills. After that, you need to devote some effort to being better at it. Introverts are more likely to put in the effort to prepare and perfect their remarks before actually delivering them. You are free to follow suit. When it comes to sales, for example, businesses often have prepared spiels that their employees may say whenever they are trying to sell a product. When you are first getting started, there is no need for you to depart from this script at all. You will grow more competent in the process as you continue to practise the ability, and as a result, your movements will seem more natural. Whenever you constantly work on a skill, that ability will rapidly become natural to you.

Find some time to relax when you've finished your assignment.

You should expect to feel more stressed than normal while you are working on a project that requires you to behave in an extraverted manner. As a result of this, you need to ensure that you give yourself enough time in between tasks to relax and collect your thoughts. If you are required to do extraverted duties on a regular basis, you run the risk of being exhausted by the experience since you are not being true to who you really are. It is essential for the overall health of your mind to schedule some time alone in between different undertakings.

The Numerous Advantages Of Increasing One's Self-Confidence

When a person boosts their level of self-confidence, they will experience many of the same positive effects as they do when they boost their level of self-esteem. We have reached this stage in the book when we have gained the knowledge that when a person's self-esteem is raised, it also raises that person's level of self-confidence. Since the impacts of self-confidence tend to be more noticeable to others, the advantages of having it also tend to be more apparent to others. People are often capable of concealing their poor self-esteem, but it is far more difficult to conceal their lack of self-confidence. Getting to know someone well enough to have in-depth talks with them and spending a significant amount of time in their company is the best way to determine whether or not someone has low self-esteem. Observing a person's physical posture, level of comfort, and ability to interact socially are three of the easiest ways to determine whether or not they have healthy levels of self-confidence. A person's ability to modify the results of their actions and earn respect from others may be directly correlated to their level of self-confidence. People who operate in environments that emphasise teamwork should prioritise developing their sense of self-assurance. People who are more self-assured are better able to foster an atmosphere at work that is more conducive to collaboration, one in which coworkers are encouraged to share their thoughts and ideas rather than just agreeing with those of their colleagues. In positions of authority, those who are able to articulate their ideas and perspectives in a manner that is respectful of others' sensibilities are in great demand. A greater level of self-confidence comes with a number of advantages, including the following:

Increasing one's level of self-confidence has been shown to enhance a number of aspects of one's life, including overall performance, overall happiness, social abilities, and both one's physical and mental health. Increasing one's level of self-confidence also improves one's ability to socialise.

Increasing one's level of self-assurance is associated with an increase in overall happiness.

It has been shown that an increase in a person's level of self-confidence is closely linked to an improvement in their overall performance. For instance, when someone is beginning anything new, such as a video game or a new sport, they will naturally get better as they continue to practise it. This is because practise makes perfect. It is natural for a person to begin anything new with less confidence than they would want, especially on the first day of the endeavour. However, when they begin to grow better at it, they will naturally build greater confidence when they realise that their abilities have increased because they are aware of this fact. This example demonstrates how self-confidence may have a direct impact on a person's overall success in whatever endeavour that they do throughout their lifetime. People who begin new endeavours with greater levels of self-confidence often do better at such undertakings right from the start in comparison to those who have lower levels of self-confidence.

People who work in fields such as public speaking, business ownership, the performing arts, and sports are often aware of the significance of self-confidence. They are aware that if they do not have confidence in themselves, it may prevent them from attaining their full potential in their performance. They are also aware that if they have confidence in themselves, they will be able to quickly solve difficulties and go past any hurdles in order to continue working towards achieving their objective. The manipulation of a client's mentality during a weight lifting session in the gym with their coach or personal trainer may be an exceptionally powerful technique. The goal of this manipulation is to assist the client feel more confident in their ability to do the exercise. For example, if the client's previous personal record for squats was 100 kilogrammes, the personal trainer will inform the client that their next set will be at 100 kilogrammes, even if the trainer has already added an additional

5 kilogrammes of weight to the barbell, bringing the total weight to 105 kilogrammes. When the customer is under the impression that they are lifting a weight that they have lifted previously with success, they assume that they will be able to raise the new weight effectively as well. In the event that they are successful in squatting 105 kilogrammes, their personal trainer will inform them that they have really squatted 5 kilogrammes more than their previous personal record. However, if the personal trainer had informed the client before the squat that they would be adding an additional 5 kilogrammes, the client may have been scared since they had never done it before, and if they didn't have the confidence from the beginning, they may not have been able to lift the additional 5 kilogrammes due to their attitude. This strategy is used rather often in the field of sports, and it

demonstrates to us that a positive mental attitude is far more valuable than a person's technical abilities.

How To Keep Yourself Motivated In Smart Ways

If you have ever attempted to achieve a goal or realise a dream, you are well aware that just having the desire to do so is not sufficient. It's simple to fall in love with whatever it is that you want, but getting what you want isn't exactly a walk in the park. It doesn't matter what it is that you want; falling in love with it is simple. The motivation, as well as your own personal motives, become relevant at this point in the discussion.

When you first started desiring anything, all you could see was your desire for the item you desired and the object itself. The psychological awakening to all of the challenges that await you along your chosen path does not take place all at once. Because humans are, at heart, social animals, these things occur in the sequence that they do for that very reason. We take in what we see, we want it, and it comes to us. The end of the story.

However, in real life, this principle isn't always applicable. In real life, in addition to concepts like "struggle," "competition," and "hindrance," there are many other concepts that come into play. Every single item is a smack in the face for the psyche.

The mind, which naively believed that just desiring something was enough, gradually comes to the realisation that there are a lot of other factors working against it. It starts to see the 'price' it has to pay in order to achieve the goal it has set for itself.

The motives are beginning to lose their initial charm in a way that is gradual but steady. The want is still very much there, but for some reason that is beyond my understanding, the drive appears to have disappeared. Mind you, the desire is still very much there. Suddenly, the only thing that is left is the portion where you want it. The reason for this, ladies and gentlemen, is that motivation has long since left the building.

If you remember well, the definition of motivation is that it "implies two things," namely a change in behaviour as well as the existence of a reason. This is quite clear. The moment each of these things comes to an end, motivation also comes to an end.

Now, at long last, we are able to discuss the most important and thought-provoking aspect of this whole narrative: "How does one remain motivated?"

The question worth a million dollars. How can one ensure that they do not lose track of the objective and continue to go forward without losing their drive?

The correct response is, thankfully, a lot less dramatic and a lot simpler to comprehend and put into practise. The following are a few of the most tried and tested ways that have been shown to be effective in maintaining motivation regardless of the circumstances.

1. Put the objective in writing.

How often have you begun anything with enough drive to conquer the world, only to find that less than a week later you are asking yourself, "Why did I even begin doing this in the first place?" What should you do if you find that you are unable to recall the reason? You, it is fairly obvious, are out.

We believe that if we are unable to recall a particular reason, it is most likely because the reason was not compelling enough in the first place. That, my good friend, is the first step towards falling short of one's goals.

As soon as you have a goal in mind, you should first remove all of the unnecessary information that is in the background, and then you should put down the primary reason why you are doing it, or why you plan to accomplish it. Don't leave any space for interpretation. When you look at that piece of paper and read your goal, it has to be crystal obvious, and it needs to get you where it needs to go you (in your heart)!

2. Divide and conquer has been a winning strategy for the most powerful leaders in the history of the world from the beginning of time itself. This tactic was used by everyone from Julius Caesar and the Roman Empire to the British

Empire. Then there is no reason for us not to.

The expression "Rome was not built in a day" is a well-known proverb.

It highlights how important it is to be patient and give things some time. Getting into something is simple, but getting out of it is more difficult. You first need to have an understanding of the many actions that will be required in order to accomplish your objective, and then you should break each step down into more manageable chunks of time.

Take, for instance, your decision to shed 10 kilogrammes as an example. One day is not going to be enough time to accomplish this goal using the method of consistent exercise and nutrition. In the vast majority of cases, it will not occur within the next month either.

But if you plan it out carefully and break it down into smaller, more manageable goals, such as dropping 1 kilogramme every five to seven days, you have a decent chance of losing 10 kilogrammes in two months, and maybe even more.

Therefore, the idea is straightforward. Break the process of reaching your final objective down into manageable periods. Then, one by one, you'll be able to bring down all of the tep and win the battle.

3. Be aware of and be open to any and all possible outcomes.

To sum it up in a single word, I want you to be sensible.

We lose motivation all the time because we don't realise that certain things aren't going to happen no matter what we do. This is one of the most common reasons. There is a potential weakness in our plan that might prevent us from achieving our objective. However, this does not mean that we will cease our efforts.

In a difficult test, your goal is to get the highest possible ranking. Are you going to give up just because there's a chance that someone else, somewhere, has a photographic memory and is also going to take the same test? To your knowledge, no.

In that spirit, you need to have an open mind and be ready for anything that may come your way. You could go very close to winning yet end up losing anyhow. Or you might have a good chance of losing but yet end up with a victory in the end!

Why should that be discounted?

4. Let go of the pessimists

There is an old proverb that goes, "A pessimist is someone who, when they smell flowers, begin looking for a grave!"

If someone has already made up their mind that they are going to fail, there is no one, and I repeat, no one who can help them. You may convert a horse that is losing a race into a winner by giving him enough help, but a horse who refuses to run has no future.The sickness of pessimism has the ability to transform even the most capable individual into someone who is completely worthless. Therefore, there is truly no room for motivation in a mind that breeds pessimistic thought since there is no room for it.

As soon as you adopt a positive outlook, you'll find that motivation is right on your heels.

5. Surround yourself with things that will inspire you.

It is only natural that you will experience feelings of depression if you are in the company of unhappy, moping people for an extended period of time. It's not rocket science; it's just common sense. If you surround yourself with people who are successful, happy, motivated, and full of energy, you will discover that some of those traits will rub off on you. Simply because the human mind is a mimicking machine. When the mind perceives ad, it experiences ad as a feeling. It is happy when it sees other people happy.

You will, unless you are a sadist or masochist, discover that being in the company of others who are energetic will cause you to feel more invigorated than you did before. Read books on how to encourage yourself, as well as biographies of people who have achieved a lot in their lives. Listening to music with a quick beat is also helpful in this regard.

6. Quit making excuses for yourself.

Motivation is like that wonderful friend that, when they leave the party, people start to follow them. When you feel motivated, others start to follow you.

But you assert that "No" one will depart after the party is over. Why?

Because you need the party to end so that you can start having fun at the after-party!

You need to stop looking for reasons to get out of the game and start looking for reasons to keep playing it. If you have five primary motives to begin with, you should add five more motives that will serve as "After-Party Motives." Maintain a straightforward policy. In this game, if you sleep, you lose. You have to put up the effort to get whatever it is that you want. Therefore, get yourself up, wipe the cobwebs from your eyes, and get the after-party started!

Is Having A Low Self-Esteem A Problem For Your Mental Health?

Having a poor sense of self-worth is not in and of itself a problem with one's psychological health, but the two are inextricably linked. When a number of different factors continue to have an effect on your sense of self-worth over a period of time, this may lead to concerns with your mental health such as feelings of melancholy or agitation.

In its widest sense, self-esteem may be defined as the amount of value that one puts on himself or herself. The ability to maintain a positive attitude towards oneself and one's abilities in the face of adversity, especially in circumstances in which one is being evaluated by others, is a key component of healthy self-esteem. Self-esteem may be defined as an individual's capability to keep the correct mindset towards oneself.

Adults who have a high global self-esteem are likely to outperform their partners in a number of areas, including financial success, quality of life in their personal and professional relationships, and overall job satisfaction. Issues relating to enthusiasm, drug abuse, and poor eating habits are some of the things that have been linked to low self-esteem. Even though one's self-esteem is considered to be a reasonably stable component of their personality, it is also subject to change depending on recent failures or successes, and there are also sublevels of self-esteem that are associated with certain aspects of one's life, such as participating in sports and other extracurricular activities.

In psychological literature, the concept of self-esteem has received a great deal of attention, which may be due to the fact that it is unconventional. In any event, despite the fact that its definition has been thrown into disarray, the idea of self-esteem has been subjected to a great deal of research, particularly in community surveys. Numerous studies have been conducted on the topic in relation to psychological well-being and the quality of life, as well as in settings such as workplaces, educational institutions, and recreational activities.

Concepts of Oneself and Regard for Oneself

People's identities, the things they are capable of doing, and the kinds of things they may become are all determined by the beliefs and evaluations they have of themselves. These wonderful influences on the individual's interior existence serve as an internal regulating mechanism, directing and supporting individuals as they go through life and monitoring their behaviour. It is standard practise to refer to an individual's thoughts and feelings about themselves as their self-concept and self-esteem respectively. These, in addition to their ability to cope with the challenges of life and to exert some degree of influence over their circumstances.

The term "self-concept" refers to the sum total of a person's beliefs as well as the knowledge that person has on the associations and qualities that are associated with their own personality. It is considered a subjective idea since it organises theoretical and substantive viewpoints about oneself and governs the creation of data that is important to oneself.

A self-concept's equivalents include a variety of concepts, such as self-image and self-observation, for example. It is generally agreed that self-esteem is synonymous with self-respect, self-estimation, and self-worth. Self-esteem may be defined as the evaluative and practical evaluation of the self-concept. It makes reference to the in-depth analysis that a person does to determine the degree to which he or she has positive or negative value and makes reference to the ratings that a person assigns to himself or herself in a variety of facets and fields of life.

The role of self-esteem as a preventative measure

Self-esteem is seen not only as a key component of psychological well-being, but also as a protective factor that contributes to improved well-being and good social conduct via the role that it plays as a cushion against the effect of negative effects. Self-esteem is viewed as a protective factor that contributes to higher well-being and positive social conduct. It is believed that it successfully advances stable functioning, which is evident in life views such as successes, achievement, and fulfilment, as well as the ability to adjust to diseases such as cancer and cardiovascular disease.

On the other hand, an unstable self-concept and low self-esteem may play an important role in the development of a number of mental and social difficulties, such as depression, anorexia nervosa, bulimia, anxiousness, violence, drug abuse, and high-risk practises. These issues can all be traced back to an individual's perception of themselves. The existence of these illnesses not only causes a significant amount of individual suffering but also places a significant burden on society. The next tests will demonstrate that having a low self-esteem may be a risk factor, whilst having a high self-esteem can work as a protective factor against certain health problems.

To summarise, self-esteem is seen as an important factor in both physical and mental health. As a result, achieving and maintaining a healthy level of self-esteem needs to be a primary focus of efforts to improve overall health, particularly mental health. The term "wellbeing promotion" refers to the process of giving people the power to take responsibility for and make positive changes to their own health and well-being. It is generally agreed that emotional regulation, along with general well-being, is one of the most important aspects of the concept of well-being.

The notion of oneself and one's regard for oneself are two of the fundamental elements that contribute to one's emotional well-being, and in this manner, they serve as an important focal point of one's psychological well-being in advance.

According to research conducted by Furnham and Cheng (2000), high levels of self-esteem are the single most important and significant predictor of happiness. Positive self-esteem, core values, and ambitions all seem to successfully contribute to 'prosperity', whilst poor self-esteem leads to personal disorder. Self-concept, personality, and confidence are some of the most important aspects of mental health.

research that look at stress as well as physical sickness provide further light on the protective role that self-esteem plays in a person's life. These research show that self-esteem acts as a shield, protecting a person from feelings of anxiety and exposure. This is evident in people's opinions of those who are always unwell. It has been shown that having a partner and a large number of close connections, together with a better sense of authority, viability, and high self-esteem, all have direct defensive effects on the development of depressive expressions in the chronically ill. It has also been established that having a healthy self-esteem may improve a person's ability to adapt to sickness and postoperative survival rates.

What Compels Me To Write This Book?

Over the course of the last several years, I've focused a lot of energy and resources on improving myself. These are the ways that I have prioritised my financial situation (sorry, Dad, if you're reading this; I did take some money out of my savings).

But the money spent was well worth it, much more so, in my view, than putting money down for a down payment on a home. I often hear great businesspeople remark that the best investment you can make is in yourself, and this is because it is the finest investment you can make.

In addition to that, I've signed up for a life-coaching certificate and a group coaching programme that will help me expand my coaching business. My mentor is an American author who has written books that have become bestsellers in the United States. I have a confidence coach of my own, a voice coach, a crazy quantity of books, a lot of online courses, and more. This is so that I may continue to better myself so that I can impart as much information as I possibly can.

I have a deep passion for education, personal development, and teaching others.

I can't take it when other people feel powerless over their life, especially when they have the ability to make changes.

There are certain things that are under our control, and there are other things that are not.

Our actions and choices can be controlled, even if it requires a lot of effort on our part, in contrast to the circumstances and events that are beyond our ability to influence. When an individual feels that they are unable to make decisions that will affect their own life and keeps negative ideas and sentiments bottled up inside of them, terrible things start to happen.

That is correct! People, in my experience and based on the findings of my study, are the worst at this, in the sense that we do not open up very well. In point of fact, the choice to participate in treatment, which I did, was one of the wisest decisions I've ever made. Take a look at the terrible things that people do to one other across the globe. Humans are responsible for most of it. However, the reason why individuals behave in such a cruel manner is because they do not love themselves, which then sets off a chain reaction that continues in a bad direction.

People will have a more optimistic outlook on the world as a consequence of working on actual concerns and developing their self-esteem, and as a result, they will share that positivity. It is obvious that this is not going to take place any time soon from a practical standpoint; but, I am making an effort to communicate with as many people as I can in order to assist them in developing a positive self-image so that they might inspire others to do the same.

Because of this, one of my goals is to encourage other people to work on improving their own sense of worth by sharing both my experiences and the things I do. Will it be simple, and will it take place immediately? No, it won't do that at all. My own work is not finished, and it never will be, but I am making progress. I will continue to mature.

You have to put forth effort, just as you do for other things, if you want to see any benefits.

As a result of the challenges I had with it during the last year, I became fascinated with the topic, particularly with the goal of boosting my self-esteem to the greatest extent possible. I am always expanding my knowledge of it, always experimenting with novel approaches to achieving my goals, and always making every effort to better myself.

But considering that you are going to remain the same person for the rest of your life, isn't it worthwhile to learn how to love that person and build that person up, as well as to put in the effort for yourself? Although it may seem egocentric, this is not at all about me.

By writing a book about it and getting my heart onto paper, it really helps me remember what I need to focus on, and at the same time, it helps other people to avoid letting negativity overcome them. I have the occasional struggle with my self-esteem (but it happens very rarely now because of the habits I put in place), so writing a book about it and getting my heart onto paper.

When my self-esteem was at an all-time low, I remember how horrible it felt to be in that place. Several instances include the impression that I was not respected, despite the fact that, in most cases, I was. When things didn't go as planned, I often had the impression that there was nothing I could do since I was completely helpless. Other times, I wondered why I should even bother attempting new things because no one would enjoy what I create or that I wasn't the sort of person who could ever do anything right.

I just do not have the capacity to fathom how others who have endured more traumatic events than I have may feel.

Then, of course, it might start to make a person feel guilty, leading them to question why they have the right to feel this horrible when there are so many other people who have it far worse.

But the fact of the matter is that we have little influence or authority over it.

In point of fact, I have the impression that it would be selfish of me not to write and publish this book, despite the fact that it exposes more than a few of my weaknesses.

It would be selfish of me to keep information to myself that I know at least one other person may benefit from hearing. Is it possible that someone may insult me or make fun of me because I wrote this book? If so, how likely is it that they would do so? Yes, there is a good possibility of that happening, but even if it did, only a small fraction of individuals would act in such a manner. Nevertheless, even if it just saves the life of one person, it will have been worth it to me.

Also, if someone attacked me for what I have opened up about in this book, I would know without a doubt that they have a poor sense of their own self-worth since I am aware of this. Because of this, I have an overwhelming need to publish a book so that I may share my own personal story in a way that others can connect to and grow from.

An individual who has a healthy sense of self-esteem would never criticise another person, but it is a well-known pattern for some individuals to criticise others in order to boost their own feelings of self-worth.

On the other hand, constructive criticism is something quite different; this is when others want to assist you in improving, and I always appreciate that kind of criticism. As I go back and reread this, all I can think of is the YouTube analysis I just recently purchased and on which I need to take immediate action. Although there was a lot that I needed to work on to become better (more in terms of design rather than what I say), I really enjoyed getting comments on how I might get better. I am aware that there is always room for improvement and I accept genuine constructive criticism that can help me get better. Because I was so self-conscious growing up, I used to despise it if somebody said anything even somewhat critical to me.

Let Go Of The Need To Be Perfect

Perfectionism and low self-esteem go hand in hand with each other. What? What exactly am I referring to? How may perfectionist tendencies go hand in hand with poor self-esteem? Let's take a look at it, along with the reasons why perfectionism causes so many issues.

Is it thus unhealthy to strive for perfection? Is it a terrible thing to want to be the best at what you do and to be the greatest? In reality, perfectionism is a sign of poor self-esteem, anxiety, and uncertainty about one's own abilities. Perfectionism may be harmful, particularly for those who already struggle with poor self-esteem. Therefore, having poor self-esteem may lead to perfectionism, which in turn prevents the individual from embracing themselves as they really are.

People who struggle with poor self-esteem are more likely to be perfectionists because it prevents them from understanding that they are enough just as they are. The pursuit of perfection suggests that who you are is never good enough. Therefore, the conundrum is clear to you.

Problems associated with perfectionism and the factors that contribute to perfectionism

So, what are the consequences of striving for perfection? What are the problematic characteristics of perfectionism, and why is the desire to be perfect considered to be such a negative trait? This is due to the fact that who you are is far more essential than what you do, but the majority of perfectionism focuses on what we do. According to the concept of perfection, we can only be deemed perfect when we carry out our responsibilities without flaw. This is the exact opposite of what you would want someone who struggles with low self-esteem to go through, yet it's exactly what they need.

If you have a poor self-esteem, there is a very likely probability that you also have unreasonable expectations for yourself. The two go hand in hand. Now you just have unrealistic expectations for yourself, and not necessarily for the people around you. The perfectionist is not likely to be content with their physical appearance, their abilities and talents, their accomplishments, or their place in life. Nothing about them will live up to their own standards, and that's frustrating.

This is an argument that goes in circles. Perfectionism may function both as a symptom and a cause of poor self-esteem. It is important to distinguish between the two. The pursuit of perfection necessarily ends in failure because there is no way to achieve it. Giving up the pursuit of perfection will result in an increase in self-esteem and progress towards the realisation that it is sufficient to accept oneself just as one is.

Acknowledge and Celebrate Your Successes

Accepting your accomplishments and celebrating who you are may help you let go of the need to be flawless and enjoy who you are. Do you give yourself credit for your successes, or do you sometimes feel like a fraud because of them? What exactly is the "Imposter Syndrome," though? It is when you have a high level of accomplishment, a high level of competence, and a professional demeanour yet you still feel like a fraud. Your predisposition towards perfectionism and poor levels of self-esteem prevent you from being able to appreciate the successes you have achieved.

Imposter syndrome is a concept that was established in the 1970s by Dr. Pauline Clance and Dr. SuZanneImes. It refers to a person (often a woman) who is highly competent and efficient but cannot get over their own feelings of inadequacy to obtain a sense of their own authenticity. Imposter syndrome was invented by Dr. Pauline Clance and Dr. SuZanneImes.

Instead of doing this, acknowledge your true accomplishments and take a serious look at the world around you. What is the truth? What exactly is taking place right now? What exactly are the facts surrounding the "situation"?

Accept and Learn from Your Errors

Accepting and learning from your errors is one tried-and-true method for combating low self-esteem. This, along with everything else in this chapter, may seem to be a contradiction, but in reality it is not. Instead of having less self-esteem as a result of your errors, you will discover that you have more of it if you accept responsibility for them and make the effort to learn from them.

The idea that you should take responsibility for your errors is becoming so widely recognised that it is slowly making its way into the culture of many different businesses. Bridgewater, the biggest hedge fund in the world, makes this practise a part of the company's culture. Since it is impossible to achieve perfection, you should accept responsibility for your errors, learn from them, and even enjoy them.

The Synopsis and the Game Plan

People who struggle with low self-esteem frequently make the mistake of comparing their inner selves with the outside selves of other people, which leads to their perceiving only the negative aspects of themselves. This is due to the fact that what you see of others on the exterior is seldom reflective of who they are on the inside, and it most definitely is not how you view yourself.

• Take care of both your body and your mind by giving yourself the attention they need. If you are not performing at your best, you will not be able to accept and learn from the errors you have made, nor will you be able to operate at your best.

• "Make the Choice to Thrive." After you've finished reading this book by Ariana Huffington, find someone else to talk about it with. Huffington has discovered a strategy that helps her silence the critical voice in her brain so that she may "live a life that matters."

• You can conquer perfectionism and learn to appreciate everything that you've accomplished by practising this affirmation. Spread the word widely in all places: 5-10 times per day, you should say, "I embrace my accomplishments!"

Characteristics of a Pessimistic Personality

The negative person is someone who is often quite easy to identify due to the manner in which they interact with the environment around them or due to the most typical thought patterns that are observable. In particular, if you were to take a step back, look around, and make an effort to truly recognise them, you would most likely be able to see these seven characteristics in the individuals that bring negativity into your life. The issue here is negativity. It is something that has to be let go of, and when you look at these characteristics, you will probably notice some that hold true for you at least part of the time — do not allow this make you feel scared or overly disturbed by it either. It is something that needs to be let go of. It is natural to have these feelings sometimes, just as it is acceptable to experience those negative thinking patterns occasionally. It is normal that this occurs. Having said that, it is essential that you be able to recognise them when they are being acted out in front of you.

Worry

People who are pessimistic tend to be plagued by an ongoing sense of anxiety about many issues. They never stop thinking that something bad is about to happen, even if they are in the midst of a period in which everything is going swimmingly well for them. This is despite the fact that everything is going swimmingly well for them right now. They have the impression that it is impossible to continue in that manner and that at some point in the future, things will all of a sudden start to go wrong. When something like this occurs, you need to be able to identify the issue and find a solution to it. You won't be able to start letting go of your worries unless you have the ability to correctly recognise the situation first.

Negative in outlook

A pessimistic outlook is when a person consistently views the world in a negative light. Even if there is still something delicious left in your glass to savour, you are already lamenting the fact that the drink will soon be gone even though it is not yet finished. When one is pessimistic, they are unable to perceive the positive aspects of any situation. You are unable to determine the means by which you will be able to concentrate on the positive aspects of your life or the means by which you will be able to collaborate effectively with the people in your immediate environment. You will discover that nothing can really bring you joy, and there is always something negative associated with each situation. Even when you are engaging in an activity that you look forward to or love, you manage to find a method to make it difficult for yourself in some manner. You always seem to find a way to bring up the fact that you are sad or that something unfortunate has occurred, and you are very quick to take pleasure in being negative. This is a significant area of concern.

Complains a Great Deal

individuals who are negative thinkers or individuals in general have a tendency to complain on a frequent basis. They always have something that is upsetting them, and it is impossible for them to discover anything that they genuinely like doing at this very minute. Even at the end of the day, when they have all that they want, they still have or find a way to moan about something. Even if you gave them a cheque for $1,000, they would find something else to complain about even if you did that. "Oh, no... that's not my bank," she said. I'll have to hold off till the smoke has cleared." Oh, it won't even come close to paying my monthly costs with that... That doesn't even come close to making a dent... But thanks for your time, I suppose." Take note of the concealed complaints; these people were presented with something that was completely unanticipated and unnecessary, and yet they still found a way to convert it into something that they could complain about. That is not even close to being fair, not to mention that it is really unpleasant to be around.

They dislike novelty and are not open to trying new things.

Negative individuals, as a matter of fact, desire to do all in their power to avoid stepping outside of their comfort zone. They are reluctant or unable to think of solutions that might allow them to go outside of their comfort zone, and this prevents them from doing so. They will go to any length to justify their continued presence there, and they will never voluntarily go out of their way to experience anything else. They have no plans to move from their current location. Stuck in place. Never expanding or evolving in any way. They desire the connections that they could form with their partners, but they are unable to do so since their pessimism prevents them from doing so. Of course, this is another issue that they will complain about as well.

A failure to achieve

The pessimistic individual is uninterested in advancing their skills. They are often their own greatest adversary in this regard since they believe that they are incapable of improving their situation. They are not aware of any better options. They do not have enough intelligence. They are always under the impression that there is something wrong with them that will prevent them from being successful. They just refuse to attempt to accomplish anything at all in what seems to be a mistaken effort on their part to protest. They never make an effort to achieve anything beyond what they already know they are capable of, and instead limit themselves to only doing the things they are good at. They never make the effort to adjust their behaviour or seek out a solution to the problem, despite the fact that it poses a significant risk to not just their prosperity but also their success. They would much prefer stay ensconced in all of that negativity and allow it to hold them back than do anything else.

They Drain Everyone Else in the Room First

When you are surrounded by negative people and thoughts, it is only natural that you would feel depleted. Negative thinkers are those who are completely unable to generate any kind of positivity, regardless of whether or not this is purposeful on their part, and regardless of whether or not they are even aware that they are doing it. They are incapable of bringing either success or pleasure. Instead, their never-ending griping, complaining, and negative attitude in general leave you feeling tired and make you want to find a way to escape, which is not always easy to do.

They Put Boundaries on Themselves

Unfortunately, there aren't that many negative individuals in the world. Even more unfortunately, they are the ones that prefer to restrict themselves, rather than looking for any method that they might achieve in life and figuring it out. They are restricted in their ability to appreciate the world. They don't experience happy feelings, and they continuously bring themselves down by thinking negatively about themselves and others.

Altering Feelings Via Behavioral Modification

Keep in mind how your ideas influence your emotions, which in turn influence your behaviour. In this stage of the process, you will be concentrating on how to modify your feelings by altering the behaviours you engage in. Overcoming behaviours may be challenging, particularly if you have developed a habit of engaging in them, but it is not impossible to do so. If you dedicate a small amount of your time to doing so, you will be able to learn how to regulate your behaviours in order to better manage your emotions.

Have you ever heard of the jail experiment that was conducted at Stanford? The experiment was carried out with participation from two different groups of undergraduate students who had been chosen at random. Others were selected to serve as the prison's guards, while others were selected to serve as inmates. They were all locked up in the basement of a building that had been transformed into a mock jail, and their natural behaviour was observed while they were kept there. The experiment was designed to investigate what would happen when some individuals were given the false impression of authority, while others were informed that they had none. Participation was totally up to the individual, and it was not required of anybody. They were free to depart whenever they chose to do so. They were able to stop if that was something they wished to do.

It is essential to keep in mind that none of these inmates or guards had ever committed a crime, and none of them had ever been qualified for a position as a prison guard because they had ever been incarcerated. The imprisonment process did not result in any significant loss of power or rights. Within a matter of days, despite the fact that there was no real power holding anyone there, the prison guards began acting aggressively and humiliating some of the prisoners simply because they could. On the other hand, the prisoners were becoming depressed and were quite passive, obeying whatever they were told despite the fact that there was nothing holding them there. They did not depart despite the fact that they were free to do so. Even though just a few days earlier, they had been peers, the only thing that had changed was that they were placed in the same room together on different sides of the bars while some scientists told one group they were prisoners and the other group that they were guards. The guards became increasingly cruel as they enjoyed their perceived authority, which allowed them to demean their prisoners. This was despite the fact that the only thing that had changed was that they had been placed in the room together on different sides of the bars. The experiment was never completed since it had to be stopped before it could reach its full potential due to how intense it was getting. Their surroundings were very literally affecting the feelings that they had.

A toxic atmosphere may cause a person to have unpleasant thoughts and feelings, which can lead to depression. On the other hand, being in a joyful and calm state might result from being in a favourable atmosphere. Altering either your surroundings or your behaviours may have a direct impact on the feelings you experience. You are able to deceive yourself into experiencing a variety of emotions. You are able to alter your emotional state by intentionally putting yourself in a more peaceful condition. You are able to agitate yourself by engaging in a variety of behaviours. In the end, the emotional state that will follow is highly symptomatic of the behaviours that you are now displaying.

The James-Lange hypothesis is a particular theory of emotions that postulates that one's emotions are the culmination of a series of preceding experiences. First, there has to be a stimulus, then there needs to be a bodily reaction, followed by an interpretation in the mind, and finally, all of these components need to come together to form the feeling. Therefore, if you apply this idea to emotions, you should be able to understand how you may exert control over your own feelings. Regardless of the stimuli that you are presented with, if you wish to act in a relaxed way, taking slow, deep breaths may help you achieve this goal. You can trick your mind into thinking that you are relaxed if you physically go through the motions of being calm. If you physically go through the acts of being calm, you can mislead your mind into thinking that you are relaxed.

People who are going through anxiety attacks are given medication to take if necessary, but they are also given tools and tasks, such as taking deep breaths, reminding themselves that they are okay, and relaxing their bodies, to stop the feelings of anxiety that were previously overwhelming them. You can see the effects of this frequently with the treatment of anxiety. People who are going through anxiety attacks are given medication to take if necessary. The methods in which we behave may have a significant amount of power.

Get Yourself Some Confidence!

Purchasing confidence is yet another tried-and-true method of boosting one's level of self-assurance. It is not possible to purchase confidence in the form of a pill or capsule, since this is not what I mean. There is a good chance that I am not referring to the practise of acquiring spirit in the form of some Iron Man–like contraption that envelops one in an incredible veneer of self-confidence. They subscribe to the outmoded notion that a person's appearance may determine his or her success. A significant number of individuals also persist in the mistaken belief that one must look as if they already had one million dollars in order to achieve their financial goals.

In other words, the exterior aspects of your look are the ones that are responsible for reorganising the aspects of your life that take place on the inside. This puts it completely in the other direction, as we shall go through later. In actuality, the opposite is true. If you want to have confidence, you have to cultivate it from the inside out before you can show it to other people. You have to begin at the core of who you are as an individual and then work your way outward. Building on top of a strong base like this is how it's done. To the contrary, if you construct your identity based on how other people see you—for example, via the use of toys, gadgets, and other baubles that you purchase—then you are dependent on your exterior shell to alter your interior self. The big benefit of purchasing your confidence is, first and foremost, that it is a simple and fast process. You may buy yourself some respect by purchasing a variety of trinkets and electronic devices if you have a credit card or a profession that allows you to make purchases. Now, bear in mind that you are not earning anyone's respect by doing so. You are deceiving yourself if you believe you can purchase respect. You are just giving other people's responses more positive connotations than they really deserve.

You are essentially capitalising on the mental sloth of other individuals by doing what you are doing. They start with a sign, and then they imbue it with a variety of different meanings. For instance, if you drove into the parking lot in a brand-new Ferrari, people would first glance at your vehicle, then look at you, and make a variety of snap judgements about the link between the two of you. People are quick to leap to the conclusion that you are a winner, that you have made it, that you are the top dog, and that you are a leader when they see you driving a vehicle that costs several hundred thousand dollars since it is quite unusual for someone to drive a car worth that much money.

It is possible, as you can well guess, that all that happened was that you borrowed the Ferrari of a buddy. It's possible that you're a technician working on that Ferrari and you're merely putting it through its paces by driving it around town. On the other hand, individuals are psychologically slothful. They accept a sign at face value and instantly put all kinds of meaning onto it, often drawing from their lack of self-confidence. Nevertheless, this method of conveying assurance is both fast and uncomplicated.

Now, there is a significant drawback to using this approach. To begin, there is a monetary investment required. The higher level of self-assurance that you want to convey, the greater the financial investment that will be required. For instance, if you ask your friends from high school over for a drink at your house and they show up at a mansion, the cost of purchasing that mansion is going to be quite a deal more than you first anticipated. Two, you are putting on quite the show here. You are conducting your life in accordance with the expectations of other people. In other words, the fact that people are interpreting meaning into what you are doing is the return that you are looking for. It has nothing to do with what you have created for yourself and by yourself. It is completely unrelated.

You have to put up with appearances even if this is already very difficult for you. You have to realise that people only offer respect reluctantly, and for a lot of individuals, nothing would make them feel better than to watch someone who they consider to be superior to them slip up and collapse. You have to realise that people only give respect reluctantly. This, of course, results in a significant increase in levels of stress.

In addition to this, you have the underlying sensation that you are a liar or an imposter. You have the impression that now that you have acquired the outward manifestations of self-confidence, it is only a matter of time until other people discover the truth about you. The level of tension caused by this is enormous. This may put a significant amount of stress on your nerves. You have brought this upon yourself, unfortunately, when you believe that your trinkets, financial goods, and other outer trappings ultimately determine who you are. If you are unable to keep up with the costs of maintaining appearances, then this is going to be an issue for you. When others start seeing you differently as a result of your change in luck, it may have a negative impact on both your sense of self-respect and your self-confidence.

Confidence in oneself and the ways in which it might influence one's work life

individuals have the ability to reach more substantial levels of accomplishment if they exhibit traits of confidence in their personalities. Confidence may benefit individuals. Because of this, they are motivated to attain not just the goals and objectives they have set for themselves in life in general, but also those they have set for themselves in their professional lives. Even though it is conceivable for people who struggle with low self-esteem to accomplish quite a lot in their lives, the main distinction is that these individuals just do not have what it takes to take pleasure in their successes and achievements. They have a mentality in which they can never have enough of anything, which, in the long run, leads to their being workaholics. It is possible to argue that a person's self-esteem is the single most important factor that not only propels them towards success but also enables them to take pleasure in their accomplishments.

The simple truth is that if you want to do anything worthwhile in life, you are going to have to put yourself in harm's way in order to do it. Have you ever given any thought to the question of what it is that motivates one individual to get up and take a step forward while another person is always being kept back? CONFIDENCE IN YOURSELF! Even if we wind up failing in our leadership positions in the long run, the confidence that we have in ourselves is what enables us to go out of our comfort zones and take on those responsibilities in the first place. The degree to which we have trust in ourselves is the single most important factor that distinguishes those who are successful from those who are not.

Many people throughout history have been successful for the simple reason that they have considerable amounts of self-confidence. This is true of both men and women. Because of this one factor in particular, they were able to take charge of their life and throw off the constraints that were put on them by a stable and well-paying work. As a result, they were able to realise their aspirations of being able to launch their very own company and become successful in doing so. Naturally, the only thing that offered these apparently average individuals the ability to escape their nine-to-five routine and instead become successful and wealthy business owners was the faith that they had in their aspirations and, for the most part, their personalities. This was the only thing that gave them the opportunity to become successful and wealthy business owners.

It is vital for you to present yourself as someone who has a natural level of self-confidence if you want to earn attention, be recognised, and be seen around your workplace. Everyone who wants to be successful in their jobs should work on improving their self-assurance. There is not another option available. You don't believe me, do you? First things first, let's take a long hard look at your company; what do you observe? It is certain that those that are successful have personalities that are filled with self-assurance and that they are able to exhibit this confidence effectively.

The reality of the situation is that in today's world, each and every firm has a propensity to have its very own culture. Because of this, it is important that your degree of self-assurance accurately reflects the manner in which other workers at your place of employment demonstrate their self-assurance. In addition, the kind of dynamic universe in which you work in these modern times is going to provide you with a never-ending stream of shifting circumstances as well as a limitless number of challenges. Your self-confidence will serve you well at times like these and be one of the primary factors in determining whether or not you are successful. I want you to know right off the bat that this is not going to be an easy task. However, if you have confidence in yourself, you will be able to keep your cool and deal with whatever problem has arisen in the most professional way that is feasible.

One other thing about having self-confidence in the job that you need to be aware of is that it enables you to concentrate and work on things that are generally far outside of your comfort zone. This is something that you should be aware of. It is quite simple to conform one's behaviour to a predetermined pattern and to feel at ease with established patterns of behaviour at work. But if you have the correct amount of self-assurance, not only will it be simple for you to move things ahead, but it will also be easy for you to work outside of the boundaries of your comfort zone. The most wonderful aspect is that you would be able to do all of this while maintaining the highest level of poise.

People that are self-assured tend to have the greatest levels of success, and this is a proven truth that no one in the whole world can dispute. These kinds of people have the potential to develop into models that the rest of the staff at the company looks up to and emulates while they are at work. Because of your self-assurance, it is likely that you may make it practicable and relatively simple for other people to adjust to shifting conditions and scenarios if you were to take this step. Therefore, if you want to differentiate yourself from the other employees at your place of employment and stand out from the crowd, make sure that you bring your self-confidence to work with you and push things to the next level! In a relatively short period of time, you will begin to enjoy the advantages, become recognised by your employers, and start to get promotions, new and interesting duties, and eventually a larger income as a result of your efforts.

The modern world is dominated by intense rivalry. In this environment, having confidence in oneself is more than just an advantage. It establishes the groundwork, which ultimately results in the formation of the foundation for your entire survival. Keep in mind that gaining a certain position in your professional life is contingent upon being asked to an interview, and while inside the interview room, you will need to show that you possess the required talents to make you competent of carrying out the responsibilities that will be set for you. In the context of the interview, it is never simple to determine whether or not you have the self-assurance to express yourself in this manner; yet, it is crucial that you at least seem confident. The moment you get that phone call telling you that you've got the job is the moment when you will unavoidably start to earn people's trust. Later on, when it comes to obtaining a rise in income, you will once again need to exhibit confidence at work in order to demonstrate that you are deserving of it. Those who are able to maintain a positive outlook are, however, the only ones who get rewarded for their efforts at work. It is the attention that they get that is solely responsible for bringing appreciation and acceptance to them, and it is this acceptance that provides them both tranquilly and an abundance of energy, which, as a result, plays a key part in their total effectiveness. You are able to become an achiever because of the efficiency that is produced via your self-confidence. Furthermore, in the long term, the successes that come your way have the knock-on effect of adding to your self-confidence.

Maintaining one's self-confidence is analogous to keeping a magical spiral going. You ask why, don't you? Because when you have a whole new level of confidence in yourself, money and happiness are not too far behind you, here is why. Because of this, it is very vital for you to have the utmost confidence in yourself; all you need to do is reassure yourself that you have the capacity to do anything in the world, and everything will turn out beautifully.

Simply because, at the end of the day, the people who believe they have a chance to win are the ones that really do!

Acquire A Sense Of Your Own Value.

Knowing how much money you have in the bank has little to do with understanding your self-esteem; rather, it is about you as a person and how you carry yourself throughout your daily life. We treat others with respect, love, and consideration; but, how often do we treat ourselves with the same regard, love, and thought? Your level of self-esteem is directly proportional to the degree to which you believe in yourself; in other words, your level of self-confidence determines the extent to which you actually value yourself.

Strong confidence is what drives autonomy, fulfilment, adaptability, the capability to adjust oneself effectively to change, co-activity, and an upbeat point of view towards any condition. Sound confidence is what motivates it. An undesirable or low level of confidence, on the other hand, pushes simply too senseless contemplations, depression, fear of the new, inflexibility, preventiveness, and an overall negative point of view.

If we are happy, smiling, and full of certainty, then others consider us to be somebody they want to be near; if we respect ourselves and depict this, then others will respect you as well; after all, how might you request respect from others if you don't regard yourself? Consequently, locating and enhancing your sense of self-worth is integral to the process of growing your level of self-confidence.

A healthy regard for oneself

If you have a high level of self-confidence, you will see certain qualities in yourself and how you see yourself. Some of the characteristics that are associated with having a high level of self-confidence or self-esteem are as follows: • You are secure about what your identity is and believe in your capabilities. • You allow yourself to demonstrate your genuine feelings to other people. • You don't have difficulty developing a close relationship with someone. • You can recognise and invest wholeheartedly in yourself for your accomplishments.

Low regard for oneself

If you have issues with self-esteem or low confidence, then you will follow a specific pattern in your considerations and ways. If you have issues with low confidence, then you will see the following focuses in yourself: • You lack confidence in yourself and are extremely unreliable. • You have issues appearing and tolerating closeness seeing someone. • You never let your actual sentiments be known.

Increasing your sense of value to yourself

Here are a few pointers for developing and enhancing your self-esteem that may help you make the most of the many methods available to you for bolstering your self-assurance and transitioning to a more gradually optimistic and wholesome perspective about yourself.

- Refrain from acknowledging the analyses of other people groups; instead, pay attention to what these groups are saying and learn from it.

- Make sure you give yourself plenty of time to relax, think, and gaze inward on a regular basis. Once you've done so, try to comprehend all of your correct assertions and visualise transforming your incorrect assertions into more positive ones.

- Recognise and honour yourself for even the most little of your achievements, and do so with pride.

- Make it a habit to engage in an activity that brings you joy on a regular basis, such as going for a walk outside when the sun is up or having an air pocket shower.

- You should never deny yourself anything that you like, and if you know that you shouldn't do it, you should do it anyway and stop berating yourself over it. • You should never deny yourself something that you enjoy.

- Engage in forceful conversation with yourself, and go through positive affirmations, in order to dispel the vast majority of unfavourable thoughts and feelings.

Changes In Lifestyle To Foster Empathy

Alterations to your way of life, in addition to adding contemplative practises into your daily routine, may help you make the most of your talents while minimising the energy-draining impacts it has on you. These alterations can be made in addition to the decision to include meditative practises into your daily routine. To get you started, here are some straightforward concepts to consider:

To begin, you should stay away from folks whose energy are negative for you. There are certain individuals who will deliberately create drama in their life, and these are the kind of people you should avoid as much as possible. Make an effort to surround yourself with individuals that have a positive attitude, as well as those who are reliable and confident.

Another thing that you should try to stay away from is any sort of media that has a negative impact on you. Unfortunately, this also applies to novels, since there are particular titles that are known to cause many empaths to experience negative emotions.

Before investing money on a book or seeing a movie, it is in your best interest to do some preliminary study on the subject. This will enable you to avoid throwing away money on something that you won't end up like. Reviews would be of great assistance for this particular aim.

Spend as much time as you can outside in the fresh air and natural surroundings. Plants are excellent emotional buffers, and being in a setting with plants automatically puts you in a more calm and collected frame of mind. Give yourself more opportunities to get away from it all, even if it's simply for a day trip to the countryside or a stroll around a nearby park or garden.

You should not be frightened of fending for yourself in various situations. The majority of empaths find that they are able to recuperate more quickly when they spend time alone. However, some people find being alone quite uncomfortable and others find it incredibly relaxing. Consider the reason why you feel uneasy in this situation, and then make an effort to get more familiar with this aspect of who you are. Your mental state will be grateful to you for doing so.

Increase your awareness of the locations that you visit that are detrimental to your overall energy level. Because this is unique to each empath, you will need to increase your awareness and, if at all possible, steer clear of certain environments. Explain to your friends why you are unable to spend a significant amount of time there, and provide some alternatives that they may like better.

If you express your demands to them in sufficient detail, they should be able to quickly comprehend the discomfort that you are experiencing as a result of being in that atmosphere.

Strive to become more adept at dispute resolution. Conflict is unavoidable, and it is quite likely that you will never develop a taste for it. You may, however, begin to exercise more control over it. For this particular reason, the assistance of a counsellor would be beneficial; however, if you would rather attempt to find a solution to the problem on your own, then there is an abundance of self-help literature available that might offer you with more insight into the situation. Do some research, and you will quickly locate precisely what it is that you need.

The majority of empaths have a tendency to choose careers in which they are able to be of assistance to others, such as teaching, counselling, coaching, and healing. It is essential that empaths working in these specific professions keep in mind the need of practising self-care.

Figure out how to put your energy to good use for yourself. You're going to have greater results at work as well!

Take a look around your immediate surroundings. Is there a system in place for everything? Is there a lack of muddle there? A tidy setting is conducive to maintaining mental clarity. Maintaining order in your immediate environment should always be a priority for you. This reduces the number of things you need to be nervous about and gives you a peaceful environment in which your mind may relax and recuperate from the stress of the situation. Keep in mind that your house ought to be your safe haven, thus you need to behave in an appropriate manner there.

One truth is as follows: An "emotional hangover" is something that will always be a possibility for empaths, no matter how much they try to put distance between themselves and those who feed off their energy.

Negative energy has the tendency to stay for a great deal longer than other types of energy, which might leave an empath feeling unwell or clouding their thinking. In some circumstances, and particularly if an empath interacts with energy vampires on a regular basis, it might take a significant amount of time for them to regain their strength.

So, in this predicament, what options do they have? First things first, they need to rid themselves of the negative energy. Emotional hangovers may be alleviated in a variety of ways; the most effective method, however, will rely not only on the circumstances but also on the particular person's requirements. To assist you in gaining a better understanding of this concept and to provide you with some guidance about the treatment of emotional hangovers, the following are a few techniques to get you started:

Advice for Overcoming the Effects of an Emotional Hangover

Meditation in the shower

Use the time you spend in the shower to assist cleanse you of any bad energy that may still be lingering. If you have enough time in the mornings or on the weekends, this is a great thing to do. Recite the following affirmation while you stand under the shower head and let the water to run from the top of your head all the way down to your feet: "This water will cleanse all of the negative energy from my body, my mind, and my spirit." while the water runs down from your head to your feet, it will have a cleansing effect on all three aspects of your being. Imagine all of that negative energy flowing out of you as you continue to repeat the phrase. Continue doing it until you start to feel less weighed down. At the conclusion of it, you will feel noticeably refreshed on a far deeper level.

In order to further purify your area and customise it to better suit your requirements, you may find that employing salt lamps and negative ion generators is helpful. What these would do is generate negative ions, which would then clean the environment of various pollutants like mould spores, dust, pollen, odours, viruses, cigarette smoke, and many forms of germs. These would be cleared away by the negative ions.

Turn on a candle that is white in colour.

You'll find that this is particularly helpful during meditation or when you're just trying to relax at the end of a hard day. This not only helps remove negativity from your surroundings, but it also produces a vibe that is more peaceful.

The practise of aromatherapy

Take use of aromatherapy's calming benefits as often as possible. Rosewater is a favourite among many people;

nevertheless, you should choose the fragrance that makes you feel the most at ease. You may choose to make use of sprays or synthetic oils, both of which must be added to diffusers in order for the fragrance to be dispersed. You also have the option of selecting cleansing aromas, such as frankincense, myrrh, or sage.

Mother Nature

We have previously established that spending time in natural settings may be quite beneficial when trying to bring oneself back down to earth. Earthing goes a step farther than this and truly links you to the ground. To begin, you will need to remove your shoes and stand barefoot on the surface of the earth. Carry out this activity at the same time as you are engaging in both visual and breathing meditation.

You'll discover that clearing your mind of any negative ideas requires doing nothing more than concentrating on the sound of your own breathing for a while. The longer you remain anchored to the soil, the more your own natural energy will be replenished by the energy of the earth itself.

Make your own little haven.

It is essential to provide a secure environment for oneself, even if you share your home with other people. If you want to meditate effectively while minimising the impact of any potential distractions, you'll need this. It does not necessarily have to be a full room. Even a nook in your bedroom may serve as a makeshift meditation space as long as it is outfitted with the essentials, such as incense, candles, flowers, and a totem on which you can fixate your attention as you practise the art of mindfulness.

When is the best time for you to put some of these suggestions into practise? There is no need that there be a "time" for it. These are essentially little adjustments to your lifestyle that you may do on a day-to-day basis. Things that you may resort to anytime the emotional hangover starts to seem like too much of a load for you to bear.

As an empath, you'll notice that this occurs rather often for you. Therefore, rather of taking action just when the issue manifests itself, constantly remain one step ahead of the scenario and prepare for it.

Developing An Optimistic And Upbeat Attitude

It is difficult to provide a precise definition of the term mentality since it refers to such a complicated way of thinking and behaving. Mindsets may be self-assured or they may be unproductive. This content is all about learning to alter your thinking after first seeing it, and it will teach you how to do so.

Although your mental make-up is continually shifting and reacting to the circumstances of each moment, many aspects of it are quite automatic. This is one aspect of the dualistic predicament that we all find ourselves in. We need to acquire the skill of striking a balance between one component and another component. For instance, let's say you've got the drive to succeed and you end up landing a position as a junior attorney at a law firm in your town while you're just starting out. When you know that you are liked by others and that you are excellent at what you do, you have the greatest confidence. On the other hand, your drinking is starting to get a bit out of hand. You wake up in the morning, put in your time at work, and leave with the satisfaction of knowing that you performed well. This is the correct frame of mind. You are now sitting there, reflecting on the successful day you have had so far. The moment you walk out the door, a shift occurs in your mentality. You give in to your laziness, go home, and start opening that bottle of wine. You have now reached a state of mind that is in no way conducive to good mental health. You have to train yourself to maintain your equilibrium. There are some mentalities that we are unable to recognise and have a difficult time combating.

You should immediately begin considering the means by which you might effect a full and fundamental shift. The issue is, when you want to make a change in your life, if it is a significant one, you will need to put a lot of intention towards it. This is the case whether or not the change will be a large one. Because of this, even a seemingly little change in one aspect of your life might result in a sweeping change in another. You need to set your sights high, much higher than you believe you should set them, in order to be able to make adjustments. This overcorrection is what is required in order to get the desired result of a little amount of change. You have to put yourself in the mindset that you will need to shoot much more above where you now are.

This is due to the fact that changing your attitude in order to entirely reprogram it is something that is extremely difficult to do, and it requires you to have a broad viewpoint. To change your mentality, you will need to get a diagnosis and take a ruthlessly honest look at what you are doing to change it.

Train yourself, for instance, to always be searching for ways in which you may grow in the area of emotional maturity if it is something you want to work on. You have the ability to reprogram your thinking so that it is geared towards change and bitterness, and if you do so, you will have a higher chance of achieving the objectives that you have set for yourself. If you want to be more emotionally mature, you should take the time to recognise, in a kind and kind manner, the ways in which you have shown emotional immaturity in the past.

It's possible that nothing will stay without first going through a really traumatic event. An encounter of any kind, from the purely beautiful to the purely natural, may be therapeutic. Catharsis may also be achieved by a thrilling encounter at a sports event, or even through sexual activity. You will need to be motivated to make the change, but a moment of catharsis may serve as a catalyst for change and help you reprogram your mentality. Entropy is something that already exists alongside humans. We are not fans of change; instead, we prefer to do things at our own pace and ignore the fact that everything is transient.

Every single one of our mental states is just temporary till the moment we pass away. That is something that cannot be avoided. Remember that even though you're having a good time right now, you may be in a terrible mood very soon. This may educate us to not let ourselves get too attached to any one specific emotional state. We need to be doing nothing more than just surfing the wave of the experience that we are having emotionally. Confidence is a component of the shift in mentality that is required in order for this to take place. As was just said, confidence might be the deciding factor in whether or not the reprogramming of your thinking is successful. It is the factor that will decide if you are successful in whatever it is that you are attempting to do or whether you need to readjust your objectives.

People who are working to pull themselves out of despair often find that they need to shift their mentality. This is a condition caused by a chronic ailment that leaves you feeling depressed and unable to inspire yourself. It causes a significant number of individuals to live their lives beyond the normal constraints of interaction and engagement with other people. People who are sad tend to withdraw from the outside world and take no action because they are unable to muster the energy to do it. Depression may be defined as a lack of desire and inability to take any action. A person with depression may change, but only if they take action and find the drive to do so.

A person who suffers from depression should try to alter their mentality in the methods that are outlined in this paragraph. They must first come to terms with the fact that they are depressed, and that this is a medical illness that requires treatment. Admitting that you need to change and that there is an issue that you are going to deal with is obviously the first step on the road to recovery. I applaud your efforts. You are aware that you are a decent person; but, you have this psychological or physiological issue that has to be addressed before you can begin to feel better. Going to see a therapist, getting more exercise, or doing any other activity that will assist improve your mental condition are all examples of possible solutions. However, the first step is for you to admit that there is a problem.

After that, after you have admitted that it is true, you can begin to formulate a plan for how you are going to address this specific circumstance once you have done so. In point of fact, there will be a one-of-a-kind approach to treating the condition of each individual, individualised to their likes and dislikes. A person who suffers from depression will need to retrain their thought patterns to move away from passivity and negative thinking. The concept of hope will play a significant role in the process of reprogramming the mind of a depressed individual. If a person is able to find even a glimmer of optimism in their predicament, they may discover that the passing of time is less difficult for them and that they have a more positive view on the future.

A significant number of individuals struggle with depression. On the other hand, some persons struggle with long-term emotional states that are comparable to depression but vary in a categorical sense from the condition known as depression. The feeling of loss is one among them. Grief is a multifaceted kind of trauma that centres on individuals, and those who go through it are forced to find a way to vent their emotions. When a person loses something or someone that they are unable to function successfully without, they are likely to be filled with sadness. A great number of individuals have been impacted to the point of suffering. Tragedy may be caused by significant occurrences, such as the outcome of a presidential election or a natural calamity. Grief is a process that requires you to retrain your brain so that you can accept the path that the grieving process will follow, regardless of what that path may be. There is often a progression of phases associated with grieving.

Having A Healthy Sense Of Self-Worth Makes One More Resilient In The Face Of Adversity And Pressure.

Studies conducted in a scientific setting have shown the connection between a good sense of self-esteem and an overall lower level of stress experienced by a person. Since a person's level of self-esteem has a direct influence on their level of happiness, it also plays a significant role in how they feel about their lives. If a person feels confident in their capacity to triumph over a difficulty that they are facing, then they will be able to see challenging circumstances as challenges rather than as threats. On the other side, if a person lacks confidence in their own capacity to deal with challenging circumstances, they are more inclined to see such circumstances as dangerous. The capacity of a person to believe that they are competent and have access to resources is what the dictionary refers to as self-efficacy. Self-efficacy is another significant factor that contributes to stress management and plays a part in one's level of self-esteem.

Because there is a demonstrable connection between high levels of stress and low levels of self-esteem, the two often reinforce one another and manifest themselves in a variety of ways. When a person has poor self-esteem, it increases the likelihood that they will have more adverse psychological experiences, which in turn makes them more prone to experiencing emotions of stress. A person with a good self-esteem who is dealing with a lot of persistent stress over a substantial amount of time in their life might actually have their self-esteem decreased over time. This can happen even if the person has been dealing with stress for a long period of time. On the other hand, a one with a good sense of self-esteem is able to use it as a defence mechanism against stress, whilst those with a poor sense of self-esteem find comfort in situations with lower levels of stress.

A "sense of pressure and/or worry" is what is meant when we say that someone is stressed. One thing that people need to realise is that the actual conditions of a scenario are not the only element that determines the amount of stress that a person is experiencing; rather, the amount of stress that a person feels is determined by how that person perceives the facts of the situation. Let's use the example of someone who is shifting houses for this discussion. Moving to a new house can be something that person A views as an exciting chance to try new things, while person B might see it as something that will be a significant source of stress for them. Person A has a higher level of self-esteem than Person B, and Person B has a different opinion of their own mobility, which both contribute significantly to the disparities in how the two see the world.

People who already struggle with poor self-esteem suffer additional harm as a result of the correlation between stress and self-esteem. These individuals often experience negative feelings such as helplessness, powerlessness, and incapability in their daily lives. They believe that they are incapable of overcoming obstacles and have a tendency to believe that any activity, regardless of how tough or easy, is unattainable; even ordinary day-to-day activities seem to be challenging for them.

Move In The Direction Of Motivation

There are a lot of different ways to look at personal motivation, or the lack of it, as well as other people's motivation. People often ponder the reasons behind their own lack of motivation or the motivation of others.

The question "How can I motivate my team?" is one that managers ask themselves very often. The issue is that they try to fix it with a simple solution, like a day of team building, and they have the unrealistic expectation that it would work like magic.

They believe that if they wave a magic wand over themselves, they will become driven in some mysterious way. Even if you hire the most well-known motivational speaker in the world, you probably won't get much more than a temporary boost as a result of their presentation.

In most cases, it does not lead to the team feeling more motivated to work together as a unit. Why? Because if there is not a distinct reason, a theme, for the individuals who make up that team, nothing will have much of an effect on them. The same may be said regarding one's own sense of motivation. Instead of just being clear about their goal or reason, many individuals spend their time looking for a magic formula that would magically motivate them.

What's In It For Me?, or WIIFM for short.

In most cases, we are not motivated in any way until the most fundamental questions are answered: Where is the value in that? I don't understand why I should be doing this. What are the benefits to me? What does this have to do with me?

You need to see some benefit to what you're doing in order to maintain your motivation. Even if your motivation is to help others, doing so will make you feel good; it will give you a sense of purpose and happiness. You need to create something and have a good reason to continue putting in effort continuously. Why else would you put in the effort and, in general, refrain from doing anything else that you could like doing instead?

When you were in school, did you ever question why you had to study certain topics if they weren't very interesting to you? Most likely, the response was "because it is a required part of the curriculum." Have you found that this encourages and inspires you to do well?

Even though you most likely complied—and since not doing so most likely had a negative influence—it is very unlikely that you approached the task with feelings of enthusiasm, eagerness, and excitement.

But I am making an effort.

How effective is it when you believe that you 'should' stop smoking, 'should' lose weight, 'should' drink less, or 'should' exercise more, even when you don't actually want to do any of those things? Have you ever come across a person who is working hard to kick their smoking habit? Give a definitive answer to the question "Do they smoke, or do they not smoke?" The issue is with the connotation that is attached to the term trying.

You are not really motivated or committed, but you are attempting something, therefore the word trying means that you are having a go at it. Only when you recognise a compelling reason and make the decision to act on it will you have the motivation necessary to alter your routines and accomplish what it is that you have set out to do.

You may put in as much effort as you want, but if you don't have a choice to back it up and a compelling reason why you should, you probably won't be successful. You can't expect to achieve this goal by any amount of teambuilding activities, inspirational speakers, or programmes. If you don't personally recognise a pattern or a compelling reason why, then receiving a reward won't help you become more motivated than just compliance.

The greater the number of themes, the stronger the motivation.

In general, the more reasons you have to do anything, or the more rewards there are for you, the more likely it is that you will be motivated to do whatever it is that you are doing. No matter how many reasons other people give you or how hard they try to persuade or influence you, you simply cannot and will not be motivated unless it resonates with what is important to you, or, to put it another way, with what you value. This is true regardless of how many reasons other people give you or how much they attempt to persuade or influence you.

It is possible to get a horse near water, but you cannot force it to drink. In the end, no one other than yourself can motivate you other than yourself. Your level of motivation will increase in proportion to the degree to which your activity and goal reflect the things that are important to you.

You are not likely to be motivated by what you'should' do rather than what you would love to accomplish since you would rather spend your time doing the former. We are, of course, also motivated by something that I will refer to as "secondary motivation."

Secondary motivation refers to the feeling that you should do something because if you don't, it will have some kind of unfavourable effect on you.

If you don't exercise and take care of your body, you run the risk of being ill. The same is true if you don't file your taxes, pay your mortgage, or generate money, among other things. There will be expenses, discomfiture, or, to put it another way, pain.

The more compelling the reasons are that you can discover to do anything, the more motivated you will be to do it, and the simpler it will be. If there is a lack of motivation, it is often due to the fact that there is neither a primary nor a secondary benefit that is readily apparent.

Examine the "pay off," that is, the rationale or benefit of staying there, if you find that you are lacking motivation in an area of your life that is important to you. In passing, I should mention that you can't make the horse drink, but you may make it very thirsty!

Am I being too sluggish?

The lack of motivation is sometimes confused with laziness by many individuals. In the end, there is no such thing as being lazy since it is impossible. However, if there isn't enough of a reason to do something, there won't be as much motivation to do it. In order to test this idea, you should ask a teenager to clean up their room and observe the response they give you.

It's possible that you mistook the lack of enthusiasm for laziness and judged it accordingly. Now you should request that the teenager leave the room. Hide money in their room in a variety of places, then give them two minutes to discover as much of it as they can before you call it a draw. What do you think would happen to the youngster who is described as being "lazy"?

go up, go out there, and make it happen...or not Motivation is what will make things happen. Get up, get out there, and make it happen. It is what enables you to get out of that chair, stop putting toxins into your body, and make progress in the direction of achieving what it is in life that you really want. Therefore, from this point on, do not waste your time by calling yourself lethargic or making a half-hearted attempt by saying that you are "trying."

Instead, devote some of your time to figuring out what drives you. You will discover that there are certain things that drive you and others that do not. You will also realise that there are some things that demotivate you. No one can advise you on what should or should not serve as a source of motivation for you. People are inspired by a variety of different things, depending on who you ask.

It's OK if you want to maintain drinking, smoking, or overeating as long as you feel motivated to do so. You are aware of the repercussions, and it is entirely up to you whether or not you choose to accept them as part of the deal. Make it happen! Be honest with yourself; this is the most important thing. The fact that you are motivated and devoted to the things is the reason why you are doing them; if you weren't, you wouldn't be doing them.

You Will Experience More Joy And Contentment In Your Life.

I decided to start monitoring every aspect of my life rather than conforming to the consensus of society over what constitutes right behaviour or going along with the flow of the mob. Because of my experiences and the way the world really is, I was able to gain awareness when I started to focus more on my own decisions and less on what other people were saying and doing in public spaces.

a number of distinct beginning points for continuing on with a conscious existence.

Ask yourself what it is that you need. How often do you fail to maintain your composure? NOT have a preference on this matter? Do you not have the remotest concept of where you should go to get something to eat? Are you unsure about what you need from the menu? Do you not have any opinions? You are in need of someone to speak for you but you are unsure which lawmaker or arrangement you need? How about you ask yourself what it is that you really require? Where do you call home now? What is it that you're craving right now? It is not improper to think one's own thoughts or have certain preferences. You won't get any criticism for doing so.

Do the things that make you happy. Why not spend your time on earth doing things that make you happy rather than committing a significant portion of it to fulfilling your obligations and satisfying your desires? Do not bother going to a certain get-together of friends if you detest spending time with them. If coming to your monthly get-together with your colleagues wears you out to the point of collapse, you should stop going. Find a different way to exercise that you like doing instead of going to the gym if you don't like going there. Make a greater effort to participate in activities that you like doing on a regular basis.

Live your life in accordance with the facts of the situation. In most cases, our thoughts and the way we conduct our lives are moulded by both society and our family. What are your thoughts? Who are you, exactly? In what do you put your faith? What have you learned to be true in your life as a result of the experiences you've had? To really live your reality, you must be honest with yourself and choose to focus on the things that have an effect on you. In addition to this, it entails being truthful with other people, communicating all that should be expressed, and being true to your identity. Not concealing one's identity by wearing a mask.

Recognise your own unique identity. It's possible that you have certain flaws and deficiencies. It's possible that you don't give yourself enough credit for being as brilliant or talented as your colleague or your sister. The vast majority of these lies are the product of having spent a lifetime being taught that you are not good enough or that you lack something. You have not been broken. In point of fact, despite the flaws or shortcomings that others may see in you, you are adequate. despite the fact that you may have been convinced otherwise by other people. It is not necessary for you to be thinner, taller, smarter, or more prepared in order to prepare better food or earn more money. People in your immediate environment will constantly compare you to others in an effort to make you feel worse about yourself and their own place in the world. Make every effort not to be fooled by it. You will attempt to feel better by evaluating the actions of other people. It is important to remember not to let your sense of superiority affect how you acknowledge others.

Carry out job that is in alignment with your being. If you are engaged in work that does not stimulate you intellectually or emotionally, you should look for ways to escape it. You are free to pursue another line of work. This is a complete piece that explains the most effective technique to carry it out. If the job that you perform does not represent who you are, then you are not yet prepared to make the most significant contribution that you can to the world. Make baby steps towards escaping your day job and engaging in employment that conveys an impression of who you are while you're doing it. You may focus on your future profession or company venture in the evenings and on the weekends, in addition to the time you have after work.

Ignore the guidance and demands that society has for you. You are going to be presented with a great lot of advice and direction from members of the community, and it will demonstrate to you what you need to do in order to be happy. Find a new field of employment, get a home, get a spouse, have a kid, and so on are all things that should be done. Create a savings plan for your retirement, put money into real estate, and continue your education. The way of society is only one method; it is not the only way. You have the ability to design your life such that it allows you to focus on the things that are most important to you.

Spend your money wisely. Take care not to fritter away your hard-earned money.

Make an effort not to fritter money away on meaningless things or spend it without much consideration. Do you in fact need whatever it is that you want to get in the near future? Is it a conscientious buy that will truly enhance an enormous worth in your life, or will it be a piece of rubbish that you're gathering from a carport deal? Ask yourself, "Am I in a position where I can continue my life without making this purchase? Is this purchase really so significant?" Be conscious of how you invest something that is undeniably valuable to you: the time that you have. Ask the same kinds of questions about the time that you inquired about the money. Stop wasting your time on activities that are mindless and unsatisfying and start doing something more productive instead.

Have courage as you go. Although we can't eliminate fear entirely, we can learn to live our lives with greater bravery and find ways to face challenges head-on. Fear should first be recognised for what it is, and then it should be questioned. Is there a basis for the concern? Is there a good chance that the worst-case scenario will play out? What are the possible outcomes, and how likely are they? When you are aware of your fear, you are able to go about your life being cognizant of it but at the same time giving it a secondary consideration. Once you've overcome your fear, you'll be able to put your bravery into practise.

Repeat "no" one more time. Living a conscious life helps you to go in the direction of a genuine living that you feel compelled to live and puts the weight of decision-making squarely in your hands. Saying "no" more often is the most effective tool you have for maintaining a thoughtful lifestyle in the long run. Saying more "NOs" rather than less indicates that you do not want more of anything. Say "no" if there is a certain food or event that you would rather avoid, such as eating it or attending it. You won't be able to say "no" to the things that really matter until you keep building up your "no" muscle. until such time as you are able to say "no" to that management, that relationship, and that horrible way of life.

What Separates Self-Esteem And Confidence From One Another

There are a few variations of this term floating around. A few examples of concepts related to one's sense of self include esteem, confidence, acceptance, worth, image, and notion of oneself.

You'll often hear folks remark they have poor self-esteem or lack confidence in themselves. Now, if you enter the question into Google or study up on the topic as I have, you'll see that there are a lot of alternative responses. As a result, I've compiled a summary based not only on what I've learned but also, and maybe more significantly, what I've experienced firsthand.

A surety or faith

I often ask them, "Confidence in what?" when they tell me they lack confidence or perceive someone else lacks confidence. "Confidence in what?"

Your level of assurance might pertain to a particular facet of your life or to the manner in which you approach life in general. It's possible that you're self-assured as a writer but less so as a singer (like me!), which means that you could be secure in one talent but not in another.

Even if it wasn't always this way, thanks to my hard work, I'm now able to engage and chat with a wide variety of individuals. For instance, my general ability to do so is fairly decent.

There's also the possibility that you may be self-assured about one thing but lack confidence in most other aspects of your life, even if you are self-assured about that one item.

For example, previous employment of mine required me to offer updates during meetings; thus, I worked to improve my abilities in public speaking in order to look more charismatic throughout the presentation.

It meant that I had practised my charm tactics, which gave me confidence in delivering my lecture; nevertheless, there were occasions when I had a very poor opinion of myself. I've heard stories of really strong bosses who don't treat their workers fairly. Despite the fact that they seem secure in their day-to-day duties, their own self-esteem is poor, and as a result, they project that low self-esteem onto their employees.

Practise is the best way to build particular confidence in anything; you can get more confident with anything by just doing it over and over again, adjusting yourself to become better if necessary, and gaining more experience. Finding a mentor who is experienced in the same field as you are and asking them to teach you what they know is the fastest method to advance in that field.

However, how you feel about your overall aptitude in life has a significant impact on your level of general confidence in how you approach life. This is derived from how highly you regard and enjoy yourself, which is directly related to your level of self-esteem. It's true that getting results is the key to building confidence, and getting results requires taking action (even if you don't feel like it). Nevertheless, a higher degree of self-assurance may be achieved when you like yourself regardless of the conclusion or the consequences, and this gets us to the topic of self-esteem... It is especially crucial in instances when our actions do not provide the outcomes we want.

The Practises That Make Someone a Positive Thinker

Positive thinkers and individuals, in general, seem to have a very predictable set of hobbies and activities that they like doing in their spare time. Their ways of living are typical, yet this is not always a negative trait. When you are interacting with someone who has a good way of thinking, you will most likely notice that they exhibit several of these tendencies. You should definitely model your own behaviour after these practises if you wish to be able to think in a more optimistic manner.

The practises that you are going to get familiar with are ones that will assist you in working towards a more positive outlook on life. They are going to assist you in beginning to engage with the world that is around you in a more positive manner. They will assist you in arranging your living in a manner that makes space for optimism to enter it on its own accord. Keep in mind that optimism may be cultivated, but it can also be drawn to oneself. If you want to be a positive person, adopting some of the most popular habits that you may utilise to improve your life is a good place to start. The following behaviours can assist.

It is not a problem if you have to invest some time and effort in order to successfully obtain these great characteristics for yourself. If you had to hurry through trying to implement everything all at once and felt overwhelmed, you may perhaps make yourself less willing to put up with everything. If you need to pace yourself, then you should do so; if you rushed through trying to implement everything all at once, then you should do so. Instead, make it a priority to ensure that you are slowly incorporating those healthy behaviours into your daily routine.

A Way of Life That Is More Healthy

Maintaining a positive attitude requires maintaining a healthy lifestyle. You have a responsibility to make sure that you have a healthy life. It has been shown that those who engage in greater physical activity tend to have a far more optimistic outlook on life. They generally have a more positive perception of themselves and experience an increase in their level of self-confidence. Additionally, the act of exercising itself causes the release of hormones that improve mood. It will make you feel as like you are participating in something that is important to them and brings them delight. Exercise improves health and should be a non-negotiable component of your life, regardless of whether you like participating in physical activity or not.

Taking One's Loss and Moving On

People that are positive thoughts are able to tolerate rejection even when it comes their way. They are able to recognise when things go wrong, and they are typically able to accept whatever has taken place. This is similar to how they react when they experience failure. If they apply for something and are not selected, they may feel sad or disappointed, but they are able to accept the reality of the situation even if they do not attempt to challenge or appeal the decision. They are able to come to terms with the fact that despite their best efforts, there will be times when they are unsuccessful, and they do not allow this reality to cause them to lose sight of what is really important to them.

Using Uplifting Phrases in Your Thinking

The importance of maintaining a positive outlook is something that we have argued throughout a complete book. Your ideas will also matter, and for this reason, as well as the fact that the words you choose to communicate what you truly believe have power over you, you will want to ensure that your thoughts are tinged with optimism rather than anything negative. If you have to think about anything, you should frame it in a positive way so that you can be confident that you can, in fact, effectively acquire the outcome that you were searching for. This will ensure that you have a better chance of success. When you train yourself to think positively and use positive language, you typically find it easier to figure out exactly what it is you need to say and when you need to say it.

Abandoning "Have" in Favour of "Get"

Another illustration of this would be the use of positive language, as well as the realisation that all it takes to ensure that you are in command of your mind is a simple adjustment of perspective. When you are discussing your responsibilities, you should try to avoid using the term "Have" as much as you possibly can. Try rephrasing it such that you get something to do rather than something that you have to do. If you are able to implement this seemingly little change on a consistent basis, you will see that it has a significant and far-reaching impact. Changing the way in which you talk to yourself is all that is required for you to become aware of a shift in your overall attitude.

Keeping from Making Complaints

Complaining is something that positive thinkers make it a point to steer clear of. Things don't always go according to plan, but rather of moaning about it, you should focus on devising an alternate strategy to deal with whatever issue has arisen. This is by far the most productive course of action. Find out how you can handle things differently in the future rather than wallowing in what you have to do or feeling disappointed, and you won't have to worry about either of those things. Instead of getting caught up in complaining or ranting, which won't do anything other than maybe relieving some of your emotions, you should take a step back and consider what may be done to improve the situation in the future. What are some possible solutions to the issue that you are having? What steps can you take to determine the causes of the problem and how to solve them?

When you refrain from whining, you free up mental energy that may be used towards finding solutions to problems. Complaining is pointless and just drains your mental resources; you will always be better served by completely eradicating it from your life rather than continuing to give in to it. Complaining could make you feel better in the short term, but does it truly get you closer to achieving the things you want in life? If not, there is no use in whining.

The Importance Of Developing Good Habits For Keeping Your Emotions In Check

The first and most important step in developing emotional intelligence and empathy in general is to take an honest inventory of your own emotional condition. It's possible that some individuals are acutely aware of their feelings at all times, while others are able to spend days or even weeks without giving it any thought at all. The problem is not as basic as it may seem on the surface, despite the fact that it may be simple to fall into the trap of making generalisations on the topic of the types of individuals who think about their actions and those who do not think about their actions.

People who say they regularly reflect on their feelings might be classified as the sensitive and empathetic kind of person.

These are the kinds of individuals who naturally inquire about the emotional state of others or who are quick to offer words of support when they learn anything that leads them to believe that another person may be going through a difficult moment in their life. It comes easily to certain individuals to be aware of their own emotional condition, and this awareness may make them sensitive to the emotional states of others around them.

People who seem to be emotionally indifferent to the feelings of others stand in contrast to those who are sensitive. These are the people whose actions give the impression that they are either unable to comprehend the feelings that other people are experiencing or that they just do not care about those feelings. In the film Fried Green Tomatoes, there is a scene in which a character who only appears for a little period of time takes one of the main character's parking places and then makes a scathing comment after doing so. It would seem that this individual is the kind of person who is unable to recognise the emotional states of others as well as the likelihood that they are unable to recognise their own feelings, especially fury. People who have this kind of mentality are often regarded to lack empathy.

The contrast between individuals who recognise their own emotions and those who are supposed to not be able to is not as clear cut as the person who has their parking place taken and sobs over it, and the other individual who commits the "dastardly deed" and smiles with a feeling of callous victory. Both of these people are capable of recognising their own emotions. There are certainly individuals in the world like that, and many of us have had experiences with people like that. Because they only have a certain amount of time to show you who someone is and they have to hammer the point home, films do have a propensity to exaggerate people.

However, the truth is that even those individuals who are regarded to be emotionless and devoid of empathy may not be as cold-hearted as we believe them to be. This is due to the fact that even they may not recognise their own feelings. This topic is being discussed for a variety of reasons, but the primary objective is to provide you with the concept that the many aspects of emotional intelligence and empathy are intertwined and interconnected. Recognising your own feelings is an essential skill in and of itself, but it should be utilised in conjunction with having empathy, being able to recognise the feelings of others, being able to self-regulate, and all the other abilities that belong under the umbrella of emotional intelligence.

What we mean by this is that the usefulness of recognising your own emotions is maximised if you then utilise this awareness as a springboard to also recognise the emotions that others are experiencing. Self-regulation, which, as you may remember, refers to the capacity to stop or divert one's own dysfunctional emotions, requires, among other things, an awareness of one's own emotional experiences as an essential component. If you are aware of your own feelings but choose to disregard the feelings of others and behave in a manner that is just concerned with how you think and how you feel, then you may be behaving narcissistically, which is a far cry from demonstrating empathy for the experiences of others.

By reviewing the scenario from "Fried Green Tomatoes," we will be able to investigate this topic in more depth. The fact that a character feels angry and then realises why she is unhappy demonstrates that the character is becoming aware of her emotions. What is not made quite apparent is the current state of the other character in the story. Because the other character seems to be indifferent to the sentiments of others, we are led to believe that they are oblivious to their own feelings as well.

People have a propensity to be thrown into a huge pot together and labelled as "people who do not care about feelings," despite the fact that there are nuances in this situation that are obscured by this kind of strategy.

It's likely that the guy who is acting insensitively is only aware of his own sentiments at this same moment. Simply because you are aware of your own emotions does not indicate that you are also sincerely concerned about the sentiments of other people. In the context of emotional intelligence and empathy, the value of recognising your own emotions lies in the fact that you may then utilise this knowledge to comprehend the feelings of others, demonstrate compassion, and exhibit empathy. This was discussed in the previous section. In contrast to what the audience may perceive, the character who is callous towards the sentiments of others may in fact have been motivated by a range of internal experiences that informed the choices she made.

This person, the motorist who cuts off another car, takes their parking place, and then makes an inconsiderate comment, may have been upset because they were running late, or they may have been thrilled because they had found a parking spot and did not have to worry about spending the next ten minutes trying to locate another one. Both of these emotions, rage and elation, are completely normal responses to the situation. They are ones that people may recognise if they make it a practise to seek to recognise their emotions and pay attention to how they feel in that moment.

The issue here is that just because you are aware of your own feelings does not always guarantee that you will act in a manner that demonstrates empathy for the feelings that others are experiencing. Although narcissists are sensitive to their own feelings and needs, this does not make them nice, loving, or compassionate persons in and of themselves. A narcissist is someone who is primarily concerned with their own feelings and goals, and they behave in a way that demonstrates a reckless contempt for the feelings and goals of others. Narcissistic behaviour is detrimental and inconsiderate to the people who find themselves in the path of the narcissist because the person who recognises their own feelings but does not subsequently evaluate, comprehend, or care about the emotions of others is performing narcissistic behaviour.

This is a crucial difference to establish since many individuals believe that being able to identify their feelings and take appropriate action based on those feelings is an essential component of emotional intelligence and empowerment. However, all that this endeavour achieves in reality is excuse and foster narcissism. If someone decides that their brother or kid who was involved in a vehicle accident lately cannot come to stay with them temporarily because it would be inconvenient for them, that person may be aware of their own feelings and acting on them, but they may also be crossing into narcissistic area.

It is essential to investigate the narcissistic aspect of the process of recognising emotions since this is a pattern of behaviour that is not only incompatible with empathy but also stands in direct opposition to it. When we act in a narcissistic manner, we drain empathy not just from ourselves but also from others around us. We are the ones responsible for creating a society in which people are driven by fury, selfish gain, spite, and retribution. The ability to make connections with other people via the medium of their emotions is a key component of both empathy and emotional intelligence. If you are just concerned with your own feelings and have no regard for the feelings of others, you are not building relationships; rather, you are tearing them down.

www.ingramcontent.com/pod-product-compliance
Lightning Source LLC
Chambersburg PA
CBHW050240120526
44590CB00016B/2160